Abide

AN ALLEGORY OF TRUTH

Rocky Fleming

Prayer Cottage Publications

BELLA VISTA, ARKANSAS

Prayer Cottage Publications – Rogers, AR

"I am the vine; you are the branches. Whoever abides in me and I in him, he it is that bears much fruit, for apart from Me you can do nothing."

Jesus

Contents

INFLUENCERS
— GLOBAL MINISTRIES —

Mission: To encourage and influence individuals toward an intimate, abiding relationship with Jesus Christ through a journey to spiritual intimacy, enabling them to be a positive influence to their world around them.

Vision: To transform lives through *The Journey*, creating a culture-changing impact throughout the church and the world.

1 | The *Visit*

In most everyone's life there comes a special person, a special time, a special event, or a profound understanding of something that reshapes his life. I found all of these things during my regular visits with my old mentor, Gabe, shortly before he went to heaven. Gabe had become a surrogate father to me, and I drove from my home a couple of hours away to visit with him as often as possible. I made it sound like I wanted to help the old man with chores on his farm, but the truth was I just wanted to be with him and soak in his wisdom. I don't think there was ever a time I did not learn something new about how a man walks with Jesus by just watching Gabe live his life. He was humorous, fun, and a great cook. He was a great host. But best of all he was my friend. I learned to cook many of his great dishes using "Bessie," the gigantic old wood stove in his kitchen. We also would fish for trout in the stream on the back portion of his property, and then fry them fresh the night we caught them. I learned to plant, culture and harvest crops in his garden. My work for Gabe was educational and helped me understand the joy of working with my hands. I would carry those lessons and delights forward to my own family and friends as I grew older. The simple relational influence that one man could have on another by simply doing life together was powerful. It also helped to know how to cook and manage the farm, for my wife and I would eventually purchase it and live our remaining days there. But that is another story.

How did this connection with Gabe begin? Why did our relationship mean so much to me? Perhaps he was a father figure, a friend, a mentor? I don't know. Because of the racial and socioeconomic differences that exist nowadays, it is hard to conceive that a black man in his late eighties and a white man over thirty years younger could bridge our differences. And it was not just the obvious differences, for Gabe represented a lot of things unlike me such as his vocation, education, and life experiences. In spite of those differences, I found that his demeanor, moral excellence, and spiritual compass made me hungry for his wisdom. I wanted to be like him. There was something inside the man that could not be understood except through a biblical lens, which tells us what a man is like who walks with Jesus. I now know that what he possessed was timeless and relevant to a longing need that most people have, including this guy. The Source in him could bridge all cultures, all generations, and all races, if I allowed that Source in my own life. I wanted to. Through my relationship with Gabe, I came to understand how social and generational walls are such foolish hindrances to stand in the way of embracing wisdom from God, though it may be packaged in a person who doesn't fit our stereotypes.   Simply put, Gabe represented Jesus. The characteristics of Christ oozed from him. He was an ordinary, rural, subsistence farmer. He was nothing special to look at, but oh, how unique he was in this world.

It was late spring and time to plant Gabe's garden. The old man was now stooped and unable to do **much of the physical work he used to do, like tilling** and planting a garden. I gladly took that chore upon myself, for my wife and I greatly enjoyed the vegetables grown in the fertile patch of ground that had been developed through years of nurturing the soil. The old farm was now mostly unused for large cultivation, and only a small patch of earth was now used for Gabe's and my table garden.

As I drove down Gabe's gravel driveway that weekend, I mentally noted him tending his grapevines hanging on the trellises. He saw me and began his short walk to the house. He looked labored as he walked to his house, almost as if he were carrying a great weight. I could tell each year how age was making him weaker, and the small incline to his house now required a lot of effort to walk. Age and gravity are not good friends for the elderly, which was the case for Gabe. Even so his

mind was as sharp as ever. When I arrived and
settled in, it didn't take me long to realize that
Gabe seemed a little distant, as if he were thinking
about something other than planting another
garden.

"Howdy!" the old man cried out to me. "Welcome
home."
"Hey Gabe. I see you've already started the work
without me," I answered.

"Oh, I was just working with some old friends to
make sure they bear a lot of fruit this season. I've
been cultivating and dressing those grapevines for
years, and they have never failed me yet. But
you've got to stay with them, or they will become
wild and dense. When that happens, you see a lot
of foliage but very little fruit. All that dense growth
gives them poor air circulation, which can bring
some fungal diseases. When you drove up I was
thinking about a passage in the Bible where Jesus
gave one of His great metaphors, when He called
Himself a Vine and His Father the Vinedresser.
Each year when I am pruning my grapevines, I

think about His words and the illustration He gave. Since reading and digging into the truths that come from that passage, I have come to see the correlation and the significance of what He was saying to His followers. In fact, I have come to see that what He was proposing and what He was inviting us to is the most important aspect of a Christian's life, except receiving Him in the first place."

I thought about what Gabe had said and could see that he was thinking deeply about the passage. As the years had passed since first getting to know Gabe, I had watched him transition into a more contemplative and serious demeanor. He still had his humor, and he kept things lively with his teasing and pranks. This never changed with Gabe even until the day he died. But this day was different, so I asked:

"Gabe, I notice you seem to be thinking pretty profoundly. Can you tell me what is going on with you?"

"I don't really know. It seems to happen around this time of year when I am pruning my vines and I think of Jesus' words to the disciples. I think I get the same serious demeanor that Jesus had when He spoke those words in John 15 about abiding in Him. Do you realize He used the word 'abide' eleven times in that one chapter? Why? I think I know why. Someone repeats a word often when he or she tries to make a lasting point, something that will be remembered, something that is very important. Jesus was only a few hours away from His crucifixion. The disciples would be dispersed as they ran for their lives, and would leave Him to face the beatings and the cross by Himself. He knew it would happen, and He was not surprised when they deserted Him. He even told Peter when and how he would deny Him. He knew what they would be facing. He was in a very serious moment in His life when He spoke this passage. His demeanor was somber and thoughtful as He prepared them for what would come and how they would be able to stand up under the challenges they would face. He was saying to them, in essence, 'Don't lose your connection with Me. It will be vital for you to stay connected to Me. Above all, watch out for your souls or else you will fail.'"

He went on, "I also think Jesus looked into the future Church that would form around those men. He was teaching them that they would not be able to do the supernatural work and produce the supernatural fruit required to build His Church in their own strength and capabilities. They would need Him to lead them. They would need to have His constant presence and constant wisdom to know what to do. They would need to abide in Him, to stay connected to Him, and this would produce a supernatural fruit that only God could manifest. To me, this is why He was so emphatic about their need to abide in Him after He was gone."

I thought of what he was saying and asked, "Gabe, does this make you serious about the same thing? Are you also looking at preparing someone for what they will face?" When I asked this, I was thinking that his children and

grandchildren would be on his mind. I was
surprised when he replied,

"Yes. I think the Lord has just pointed to me to
play a part in your understanding of this passage
and your need to abide in Him. I have watched
you faithfully serve others and especially me. You
have a good heart. You are a seeker, for you
study His word to find His truths. I have watched
you become a self-feeder on God's word and not
require others to spoon-feed you. If one's spiritual
development could be started and finished by
diligence and knowledge of the written word of
God, then I think you would be a good example to
follow. However, you cannot go into an abiding
relationship with Christ by knowledge alone.
Knowledge is the way to it. But knowledge is not
our destination. Abiding in Him is our destination,
and this you still lack."

I thought on Gabe's words and felt challenged by
my own preconceived opinions that having Bible
knowledge is the greatest evidence of godliness. I
thought of some preachers, seminary professors,

Bible teachers, authors, and such whom I held in high esteem. But I also realized I had heard the words of some of these people and thought they had it all together because of their Bible knowledge, only to be greatly disappointed when some were disgraced by hidden lifestyles that were found out. I could see by the bitter fruit their lives produced that they did not know Jesus in an abiding way, and the work they did was only the result of manmade efforts and likely for show. It was obvious that knowledge alone is not evidence of a healthy soul, and Gabe's words were hitting home.

It is so easy to judge people when they fail. They are easy targets. I think people in general find comfort in putting someone else down when they make a mistake or are found to have a hidden lifestyle that is contrary to their public character. Fallen pastors and celebrities are obvious targets, but so are church leaders, community leaders, and anyone we feel a freedom to criticize.   The Lord was teaching me that if I embrace a prideful criticism of another person, I embrace some form of evil in my own life, and this in turn becomes a problem for me. For that reason, when I had just such a critical thought come to my mind, a sudden remorse came over me, prompting me to not judge these people because of their failures. Maybe I was grieving the Spirit and that is what I felt? Rather than criticize the failure of a person, I should heed the warning that all followers of Christ live lives of constant threat. A steady seduction comes at us to lead us into darkness if we will follow it. If we are not strong in the Lord and His might, we could be easily seduced and go the way of many who could not stand the tests. I could be one of them if I didn't grasp that it is not mere knowledge of God and the scriptures that helps us stand strong when tempted. It is the accountability to the love Christ has for us and our love for Him, and this is why the destination Gabe was speaking of was so important. It is a place of intimacy with Christ that creates this bond of love. I then asked my mentor,

"Gabe, how do I get there? How do I get to this abiding place with Jesus?"

He answered, "That is the message Jesus gave us in His vine illustration. Let's read it and see what He was saying, and how He would answer your question. Gabe and I turned to John 15 and read it together. He explained,

"Do you see what I mean about Jesus' emphasis on abiding? He used the word 'abide' eleven times in the same conversation. It sounds like an essential message for someone who wants to be a disciple of Christ, do you agree?"

Of course I had to agree, for the evidence and the emphasis were obvious.

"Gabe," I asked, "I have a few questions I need some answers to and I hope you can give them to me. What does it mean to abide? What is the fruit Jesus is speaking of and what does it mean to be pruned?" I got those questions out as quickly as possible for they were the first things that came to mind, and I knew nothing about growing grapes. For some reason I thought I needed to know more about the metaphor Jesus was using to understand the truth He was trying to convey.

By this time Gabe had brought us two glasses of iced tea to enjoy while we visited on his front porch. I was always amazed at how easily the old man entered a conversation with me and kept it relaxed and non-threatening, but profoundly relevant to my spiritual health. I always knew there was some kind of strategy at work when we met. Some people might not have liked it. However, I wasn't concerned, for I trusted him as my mentor. I felt that his agenda to help me grow in Christ was always for my benefit and because he loved me. I could tell this weekend would be one of those very important occasions Gabe had in mind for me.

"Son," Gabe began, "I'm an old man, and you and I both know I am not long on this earth before I will be called home. At my age, a man wants to transfer what he feels is the most important information he can share with someone he loves. I have watched you grow like a weed since the first time I saw you during that snow storm several years ago. You looked like a wet, frozen corpse knocking on my door. I knew right then that God brought you to me for a reason bigger than both of us. It was divine orchestration that brought us together that night, and God's plan has deepened our friendship ever since. There is a reason. I now see that the Lord is pointing me again to serve you by giving you the most important information I could ever pass along. It is to understand the mystery of close proximity with Christ and what that does for us. When you enter that place, you will be formed into a man after God's own heart, which is beyond anyone's expectations. If you do not go there, you will live with spiritual frustration all of your life, and you will never become the man God wants to make of you. I think God is wanting to take you to the next step, and I want to share with you what that step is."

I was totally captivated by what Gabe had said, and I wanted to know where he was going to take me next.

2 | The *Vine*

We had just read John 15 and had discussed the circumstances surrounding this message Jesus gave to the disciples. Gabe continued, "Now let's take a walk to my vineyard and try to get a little more insight into what was behind Jesus' illustration."

At that point Gabe rose from his rocking chair on the porch, grabbed a walking cane, and began walking toward his vineyard. I followed close behind, caught up with him, grabbed his free arm, and helped him down the path. I always feared

him falling if I were not with him. However, he was always cautious and picked his way carefully down the path. When we got to the trellises that supported the vines, he paused,
took a deep breath, and delicately touched one of the vines.

"When Jesus gave His illustration about the grapevine, most of those men understood quickly how grapevines grow and what a vinedresser needs to do to help it produce more fruit. It was part of their culture. They might have had some grapevines they tended around their homes in the regions they were from. They connected immediately with Jesus' metaphor. You likely do not understand how a vinedresser works with a grapevine, do you?"

That was for sure. I was raised in the city and the closest I got to a grapevine was eating a grape. I had seen vineyards from a distance but never up close. I didn't even know what to look for, whether a vine was healthy or sick, or how to help one produce more fruit.

Gabe pointed to the vines that were neatly growing on wires supporting the arms of the vine. "Take a look at my vines on their trellis. What do you see?" asked Gabe.

I looked at one of the vines on its trellis. It was late spring, therefore there was new growth. The vine started up from the soil and when it got to about chest high, it branched out with one arm of the vine going one way down the trellis, and the other going the opposite direction. The vine formed a "T," and on each arm were small shoots several inches apart projecting upward. On the shoots I could see tiny grapes about the size of BBs being formed on the stems.

Gabe said, "Depending on the variety of grape, I could train the vine to produce its fruit below or above the arms of the vine. I could also use a trellis that has two or four arms off the trunk. In this case I've used a single cable to support only two arms coming off the trunk. I determine this based on what I'm trying to achieve. In the same way, Jesus said the Father is the Vinedresser to the Vine, which is Him and His Church. The Vinedresser has a master plan for His Church, much like a vinedresser does with his vineyard. That is why you see different varieties of fruit and expressions within God's family around the world. He also has a delicate plan for the individuals in His Church. We are His family. You and I are part of His master plan and He works to form us into fruit-bearers like a vinedresser does his vine. Do you see the connection and the parallels Jesus introduced in John 15?" It then became very clear what Jesus meant.

After showing me the first grapevine, Gabe then walked me to the side of the field and told me to look at another. It was a grapevine alright, but it was nothing like the ones I had just seen. The first vines on his trellises had order and tiny fruit was already showing. The grapevine on the side of the vineyard was wild and had a dense mass of old growth. There was no order to it, and only a semblance of fruit was beginning to show.

Gabe explained, "I planted this vine at the same time I did the ones you saw on my trellises. It is the same variety. It gets the same water and sunshine as the others. It is in the same soil and yet there is a big difference with the look, and the lack of fruit it produces. It looks neglected for it has not been trained or pruned. What do you think has made the difference?"

"Gabe, it is obvious. It is your work and involvement with the healthy vines that has made the difference." I answered.

"And that is the first hidden truth Jesus was telling His disciples when He used the vine illustration," Gabe replied. "He is the Vine, we are the shoots on the Vine, and His Father is the Vinedresser. Being the Vinedresser, the Father has a plan. Just like my trellises have been planned, God's plan for us has order and vision in His mind. His plan has strategy. Just as my vines cannot know my strategy for them, neither can we know the Father's plans for our lives. However, we are told by Jesus that we are part of a bigger plan, and His work in our lives is to form us into fruit producers to join other fruit producers. The way He does it is organic, inside out, like a vine's fruit must begin in the Vine itself before it reaches the branches, and then the branches to the fruit.   This is an organic picture of Jesus to us and through us, and this produces the fruit in our lives. This is a key thought to understand Jesus' points about abiding in Him to be able to bear fruit. Furthermore, our lives are to be more than just a good life for ourselves. If we live in close proximity with Jesus in the abiding relationship He speaks of, then our life will affect many other people as His fruit is born through us to them and then through them to others. Do you understand this process?"

Before I could answer, Gabe said, "Now let's take a look at how I prune my vines, for I think it will help you understand how and why the Father prunes us."   We then returned to his trellises for a new lesson.

3 | *Pruning*

Back at the trellis Gabe continued, "Look carefully at the vine and the stubs jutting up from it every six to eight inches." I looked and sure enough there were little short stubs about every six inches laid out in order on the vine. On the stubs were green shoots, and on the shoots the immature clusters of grapes, I mentioned.

Gabe explained, "That order didn't come naturally. I started by pruning the arms of the vine to create those stubs you see. They are called spurs. The branches and the fruit grow on them. This reminds me of how prophets like John the Baptist prepared the way for the coming of Jesus. There were thousands of years of cultivation by God from Abraham to John the Baptist, and they were used to lay the foundation of the Gospel. In other words there was a lot of preparation that went on before the fruit bearing manifested itself through Jesus and the Church. Just like a vine is prepared by the harsh cuts and pruning I perform, Jesus underwent a similar process by His stripes and crucifixion to prepare the way for the Church and our fruit bearing. The Church has been formed on the wounds of Jesus, and just like my fruit grows on the wounds I give to the vine to form those spurs, our fruit is formed from our intimate relationship with Jesus. Do you see the similarity?" I nodded that I did.

Gabe continued, "After the vine is prepared by creating the spurs, the branches form on them. The new branch on the vine will now produce fruit. At the end of the season I will prune it back. Here's the key: The grapes grow only on one-year-old wood on the vine. The first year the green shoot turns to brown by the end of the season, and it is then considered "one-year-old" wood. Grapes will not grow on older wood of the vine. Older wood only produces leaves. The one-year-old wood will produce flowers and then grapes the next year. This is why a vinedresser must always prune the branches of the vine. It is so that flowers and eventually fruit will grow on a branch. I prune mine every winter, and when spring comes they know what to do. They bear fruit. It comes naturally."

As he pointed to one of the branches growing up the vine, Gabe elaborated: "By the way, when Jesus spoke of Himself as the vine and His disciples as the branches, He was speaking of those small branches on top of the spurs. He was saying that you and I and all of His disciples are like little shoots on a vine that start out green and young as His little children. He then nurtures and prunes us into mature branches, and this is where the fruit is produced. So even though we are saved and part of Him, we still need to be nurtured and developed by the Vinedresser to be fruit bearers, just like any good vinedresser would do for his vineyard. As a branch on a vine needs to be pruned every year, so a disciple of Christ will be regularly pruned. The pruning shapes the potential of the fruit on a branch for the next year, which is the same for a disciple of Christ. In the winter I cut the branches I have developed on a vine down to about six or eight inches, and I leave about two or three buds on the pruned branches. I'm preparing the branch to produce the best fruit it can produce. In a similar way God has a plan for our lives that we are not aware of. We do not know the fruit He has in mind. But He has a plan, and you can be assured that His plans are good."

I asked Gabe, "I notice that you have a different position for the branches to bear fruit on some of the other trellises. Some of the branches point up, and some point down. Why is this?"

"The variety of the grape dictates the way I develop the spurs. Some varieties grow best in a particular position; it may be below the vine or above it. A particular variety is suited for the way I have formed the vine," he explained.

"Now I have a question for you," Gabe began. "If Jesus represents Himself as the Vine, how would the different forms of trellises fit within His illustration?"

I thought for a moment and suggested, "I believe it could be an example of Christ working within different cultures and different forms of worship. We might look different from each other in our forms. Our fruit may look a little different based on what the Lord wants to grow. Our churches may worship differently from others, as several denominations do. But the dynamic of spiritual growth and the way fruit is produced is the same. We are all dependent on the Vine to be the kind of fruit bearers Jesus spoke of."

"Alright!" Gabe exclaimed. "You have just connected to a hidden truth within God's Vineyard that we call the Church! Now let's walk up the hill a little way and discuss this thought some more." With that, Gabe began to walk a short way up the incline leading to his house, and I followed him.

He wanted to take me to a point of view where I could better understand a truth often missed.

4 | The Church, God's *Vineyard*

Gabe continued his download of wisdom by asking me to take a long look at the farms around his in the fertile valley. From the new vantage point, I could see several neighboring farms. from the vantage point I had been given. The farms were active and had several fields planted, unlike Gabe's farm that had been greatly reduced of its crops. However, like Gabe's place the other farms had a few grape trellises scattered around. It was then that Gabe spoke:

"Do you see the other grape trellises on my

neighbors' farms?" I nodded that I did. Gabe went on.

"This is an example of different farmers growing different varieties of grapes but using the same methods I've mentioned. Other vineyards around the world use similar dynamics that I've shared with you to produce their fruit. But the growth principles are all the same. There are different grapes, different forms of trellises, and different uses of the fruit, but everything is always dependent on the vine and the branches having a healthy connection with each other. The pruning and nurturing of the vinedresser is required for the plant to bear the best fruit it can produce. The vine will not do it on its own. This is the illustration Jesus gave to His disciples in John 15.   It is the same way the Body of Christ in nurtured around the world. The Church throughout the world depends on the same principles that Jesus taught to bear fruit. Whether this is an individual person or a local church or a parachurch ministry, no matter the nation or culture, we all must be connected to the same Source, for our growth

and fruit is always dependent on our connection to
the Vine. Now why do I share this with you?"
Gabe asked. Before I could answer he added,

"I wish all denominations and all Christians in the
world would see that just like the different varieties
of grapes God has created, our differences as His
children are beautiful in His eyes, for He formed us
differently. We should celebrate our differences
rather than condemn them. The way the Lord
works within our lives and our churches may be
different. But it is by His design that we are
different. We are all part of His Vineyard. We are
all being nurtured by the same Vinedresser Father
to bear fruit to His glory. Therefore, there is no
place for competition or rivalry or jealousy in the
family of God. If we could learn this and accept it,
just think how God's family would impact this
world we live in. We need this message of truth
going out all over the world, and especially where
there is rivalry. We are His family. We are all loved
by our Father, and it is time that we love each
other as His family should. You see, love, the kind
of love that only God can give, is a fruit that comes

to us and through us when we abide in Christ. This is why I believe apart from our salvation, the greatest gift we've been given, and the greatest need in the Body of Christ today, is to abide in Christ and find this love connection we are given. We must embrace it for our lives to change and in order to reach a world that does not know this kind of love exists."

After Gabe shared this he changed the subject and showed me another interesting dynamic with a vine and the way fruit grows on it when he said, "Notice one more thing before we walk back to the house to discuss John 15 and the illustration Jesus gave. Look at the little fruit clusters on the vine. Where do you see the most, and largest fruit?" He asked, as he pointed to a vine on a nearby trellis.

I carefully assessed the plant and could see immediately that the fruit growing closest to the trunk of the vine was larger. As the vine grew outward, the fruit on the outside branches looked immature and behind in its development compared to the grapes nearest the trunk. I told Gabe what I

was seeing and asked him what it meant.
He replied,

"This is because the best and more mature fruit is
being produced when it is closest to the source of
nutrition. Remember the closer to the source, the
better the fruit. This is true with the fruit on the
grapevine, and it is especially true for the fruitful
lives of a Christian. The closer we are to Jesus,
the better the fruit is in our life. That is why Jesus
used the word 'abide' when He gave the
grapevine illustration. He was conveying how
essential it is for us to abide in Him to be fruit
bearers. He was saying that close proximity to
Him is the greatest concern for a Christian. Sure
He wants us to bear fruit. He said the Father is
glorified when we bear fruit, and we prove
ourselves to be His disciples. But it is not the fruit
we tirelessly try to produce for Him that glorifies
the Father and proves we are Jesus' disciples.
Actually that effort is artificial and produces only a
glimmer of real fruit, if we try to do it on our own.
Rather, it is our close proximity to Him that is of
greatest importance for it is there that the Source,

Jesus, is able to flow through us more quickly and dynamically. It is actually Jesus that produces fruit through our lives, and just like the grapevine, when we are closest to Him, the fruit is best. Remember this: We do not get closer to Jesus because we bear greater fruit. This would be a works-oriented perspective about our relationship with Christ, which can easily become legalism. Rather we bear greater fruit because we are closer to Him. This closer proximity to Him allows His grace to flow through us, and the more we receive of it, the more it passes through our lives, and it is this grace of His that becomes fruit in our lives … the real fruit that only He can produce."

When Gabe made this illustration clear to me, I could see why many of my efforts fell short of producing the kind of fruit Jesus spoke of. This is why I felt frustrated with so many ministry efforts I made. I could also see that many churches worked hard but produced very little life change in their people. We were trying to do good things using our own effort, but not from an abiding relationship with Christ and His power. Little wonder we were frustrated. Little wonder we often felt so defeated when our good intentions didn't work out.

It was becoming clear to me that the Lord had been allowing me to grow up from a tender shoot just like Gabe had illustrated, and I was now being positioned for a needed transition into a fruit bearer. Something was now more important than my personal growth, which had been my greatest concern before. I could feel that I was being invited into a relationship with Christ that was deeper than I had ever had, and Gabe was being used to shine a light on my path. I had to ask a question about all I had seen in his vineyard before we returned to his house,

"Gabe, I learned a lot today about growing grapes and nurturing grapevines. I appreciate the diligent work you put into the whole process of producing the fruit. It makes it clear why I needed this lesson to better understand abiding in Christ.

He answered, "You asked me how to go to this place of intimacy with Christ that I spoke of. I wanted you to have a foundation of understanding the vine, the branch, and the fruit from Jesus' point of view before we head back to the house and I answer your questions.

The old man began his slow return to the front porch of his farmhouse where we continued in our rocking chairs, along with some cookies Gabe had baked. I was now ready to understand the invitation Jesus gave His disciples to abide in Him, and the hindrances that get in the way on our journey to intimacy with Him.

5 | *Abiding* Defined

My mind was still spinning from all Gabe had
skillfully imparted to me about growing grapes,
and the amazing similarities to the illustration
Jesus gave. So, I led out with my first question:

"Gabe, when Jesus used the word 'abide' to
describe the kind of relationship He wants us to
have with Him, what did He mean? How do I get
to that kind of relationship?" I pressed.
"What do you think it means?" Gabe countered.
"Does it mean to have a daily quiet-time?" I
answered, while feeling pretty confident about my

daily routine. Like Gabe said, I had becoming a voracious self-feeder in God's word.

"How often do you have your quiet time and for how long?" Gabe asked.

Again feeling confident, I said, "About an hour most every day."

I could see the little twinkle in Gabe's eye like a trapper ready to spring his trap. It was always with humor and non-threatening, but I knew something was coming that would challenge my prideful words.

"Well, let's go back to John 15 and look at the word 'abide.'   Let's look at some other translations and see how they describe 'abide,'" he remarked. He then handed me another translation and asked me to read it. He asked, "What do you see this version use instead of the word 'abide?'"

I took the NIV Bible and read the word "remain" instead of "abide" in the same verse. Immediately I knew why Gabe had the twinkle in his eye. My prideful idea that abiding in Christ was simply a good quiet time was shot down before my very eyes. I knew what Gabe was going to say next. That old codger had set me up.

Again with the twinkle and hidden smile Gabe said, "I guess I'm kind of ignorant on a lot of things. But I don't see how I can abide in a quiet time if I have to remain there all day long. How can I do all this work on a farm if I have to stay in my chair and read my Bible all day? Is that what Jesus wants me to do to abide in Him … to remain with Him in a quiet time all day long?"

The spring trap was sprung as I had ignorantly walked right into it. My pride and ignorance had been exposed, and that old man had gotten me once again. If I didn't love him so much I would have been ticked off. But the problem was he was right. I remembered a passage in Proverbs 9:8 that says, "Do not reprove a scoffer, or he will hate you; reprove a wise man, and he will love you." I wanted to be a wise man, and I had a mentor in Gabe who was helping me with the process. I didn't like it, but I had to admit with a veiled smile.

"You old goat, you did it to me again!"

"Will I ever learn the way you spring your 'understanding moments,' as you call them? I think I will call them 'understanding traps!'"

Gabe laughingly said, "Good medicine, my boy. Open up for some more, 'cause the doctor is in the house."

With this last statement we both broke out laughing. We left my lesson on abiding for the time being, and we talked about the numerous other times Gabe had reeled me in like a fish on a line. Our laughter was good medicine for both of us. We would return to the front porch the next day to begin discussing some other critical things concerning spiritual growth, and especially my journey to intimacy with Christ and the abiding relationship we had discussed. However, I had another line pulling objective before the afternoon was over. I wanted to take my fly-rod to the stream behind Gabe's house and pull in some trout for dinner. I told Gabe that if I could catch the trout I would fry them for dinner. If not, I would take him to Maude Mae's Grill in the general store, down in the valley. It was just a small stop in the road, mainly catering to the families and farmers in the valley. But Maude Mae cooked some of the best burgers and fries I've ever tasted. Either way we would have a great dinner.

My time on the river was uncharacteristically unproductive. The trout had no interest in my flies no matter what I threw at them. After a while I gave up and simply sat by the stream to contemplate the information Gabe had shared with me. I got out my journal and recorded the following thoughts as I processed the dynamics of the vine and the branch,

"Abide is translated to 'remain'. What does this mean? I think it means that we do not just visit with Christ on occasions and it be an abiding relationship. We must come and remain for us to abide. How can I do this? How can I keep a constant connection with Christ throughout my busy days? Is it even possible?"

I thought on those words I had journaled for a while, and my thoughts then turned to a prayer:

"Lord, I want to truly abide in You 24/7. All I can

do at this point is say that I am willing to join You to abide more deeply and constantly in You. I understand I'm looking at a lifetime process. I don't know a lot, but I have come to understand that nothing worth doing is a quick fix. I must be committed to a lifetime pursuit of this to enter and live in Your presence. However, I need Your help to show me the way to this place that is closer to You and that which You speak of. Help me to understand what stands in the way of my abiding in You, for it is clear that the invitation has been given. Is there something I'm not letting go of that keeps me from entering into that special place with You? Give me the courage to discard those things that hinder my progress. Also, Lord, help me understand how and why You prune me. Grow me up, Lord, to bear great fruit to Your glory through my life. I am ready to go there. I ask You to lead me to my next steps."

6 | Fruit Bearer

After my prayer I returned to Gabe's house. By
this time, we were both very hungry. Burgers
would be a great treat. As soon as I stepped on
the stairs to the front porch Gabe had risen from
his chair and was turning me around to load up in
my truck. He was ready to go. We drove down
the road a few miles and arrived at the century old
building that housed the general store and the
little restaurant.

As soon as we walked through the doors
into Maude Mae's Grill, all eyes turned to look at
Gabe. People came up to greet him and welcome
him. Children came up and Gabe knew them all,

along with their parents. He asked about each of
them. He even knew the names of some of the
dolls the little girls carried and the things the little
boys were involved with. I have never seen such
attention given to someone, as these people gave
to Gabe. He was truly beloved. Until that moment
I thought of Gabe as my mentor, but I didn't know
others who knew him. I kind of thought of him as
my exclusive friend. I would come to understand
later when I purchased Gabe's farm after his
death, that many people loved him, and that he
was a mentor and friend to most of the people in
the valley. The truth is Gabe was so unassuming
and humble that I did not think of him as a power
broker of influence. Through this humble man I
was taught a much-needed lesson that Gabe's
abiding in Christ made him the friend and mentor
he was. This was evidence of the fruit Jesus
spoke of. If I needed an example of the man I
wanted to be and the one I hoped Jesus was
transforming me into, I was looking at it.

The service we got in the little country
restaurant was as if royalty had walked into the
place. The burgers and fries were as promised.

The coconut custard pie was a sweet closure to a great meal. We were both very satisfied. When I went to the counter to pay our bill, Maude Mae looked at me and said,

"Our young waiter didn't know our rule about Gabe when he gave you this ticket. Gabe will never pay for a meal in this restaurant, ever. What he has done for us and what he has meant to us has made him our hero. You will never know how he has shaped the destiny of this valley." She then took the check and tore it up.

She looked at me with a very serious stare and said, "We will always be there for Gabe. He can always count on any of us in any way."

I got a little uncomfortable for I felt she was also saying behind her words, "Buddy, you better treat Gabe with the respect and dignity he deserves, for we are watching you." I got the message and replied, "You can count on me as well. I feel the same way you do."

After we returned to Gabe's house and he went to bed, my mind was still processing the things he had taught me and the example God had set before me. Instead of going to bed, I went to the porch to look at the stars and hear the sounds of the country. The clouds during the day had faded out and had left a crystal clear sky. The stars were out like diamonds on black velvet cloth. The Milky Way was clearly visible. The whippoorwills sang back and forth as they flew closer to find each other. A coyote pack was hunting, and the shrill barks they made were echoing through the valley. Every now and then a dog would answer them, and a chorus of sounds filled the night. Sights and sounds in the country were very soothing to me compared to the city noises of my home.. At that moment I was being ushered into a cathedral of worship and I took my cue. I lifted my outstretched hands into the sky. I had nothing to ask of my Father. I only had one thought. I wanted to thank Him with the deepest part of me. I longed to say words that connected with how I felt. But I could not find them. Instead I shook my head back and forth saying, "Thank You, Father. Thank You, thank You, thank You." My words felt so grossly inadequate, but so deeply connected to my heart of worship for my King. Almost as if I felt the Lord speak directly to my heart, I had the

strongest impression that He was answering my
prayer from earlier in the day. I had asked Him to
show me the way to the place closer to Him. I
needed direction, even my first steps. I now
understood that He was showing me that my
journey must begin with sincere thankfulness.
This kind of thankfulness is driven by recognizing
who He is and what He is, but also who I am to
Him. I am His beloved son. This was the key I
was looking for. This spirit of gratitude going on in
me helped me tune in with the Lord. I realized that
it was not for His benefit that I needed to
recognize both His holiness, accessibility, and my
position with Him. It was for my benefit, so I could
begin to commune with Him with my heart, which
is my deepest, innermost being. To navigate the
choices ahead in my journey to an abiding
relationship with Him, and to keep on abiding with
Him, I needed to hear Him more clearly. This
thankful spirit opened my heart to His voice.

My night continued on with a combination
of absorbing the beauty of the nighttime sky, and
its connection with my Creator God who formed
the Universe. This led gently to an overwhelming

realization that I am indeed the Father's son. I am in His family, and He is inviting me to come closer to Him. I wanted nothing to stand in the way of this. I was motivated. But I was still ignorant of the process and the benefit. This is why Gabe was such a valuable tool in the Father's hands for showing me the way. I knew it would be my choice to make the journey ahead for me. Gabe could only point the way. But he would play a part in my journey, and I was ready to meet with him the next day and for him to show me things I had never thought of. With these thoughts I went to my bed for a good night's sleep.

7 | *Discipline*

As had been the case every time I visited Gabe, he woke before me, started a fire in his old wood stove, brewed coffee, and started cooking before I woke up. The aroma that greeted me was very special. The pine kindling he used to start his fire had a sweet rosin smell that is distinct and signifies that his kitchen duty has begun. Next, he placed oak wood on the pine to create a steady, controlled burn. As the coffee was brewed, my nostrils flared with anticipation. Like a magnet, I was drawn to Gabe's kitchen where a coffee cup full of the hot java was extended to me by my friend. He then put his biscuits in the oven to bake while frying bacon or country sausage. Eggs were cooked last and everything finished together, always hot, always done, and always good. That was breakfast at Gabe's house. Occasionally when Gabe would come to our house for a visit, my wife and I tried our best to impress him with our cooking. Though always gracious, I felt he put up with it more than enjoyed it.

I lingered in the kitchen with Gabe while he cooked. We ate and I washed the dishes afterwards. We then took an extra cup of coffee to his porch rocking chairs to continue my education concerning abiding in Christ.

Gabe started by asking me, "Did you gain understanding yesterday about how a vineyard works? Do you remember the differences between the untended and tended vines? Do you understand how important the vine keeper is in the fruit bearing process?" I thought of the overgrown, wild vine on the edge of the vineyard, and did a mental comparison to the trellised vines he tended. I answered, "I could see the difference in the two easily."

Gabe continued, "You need to consider something else about the uncared-for vine, for there is another biblical truth about discipline that leads to abiding and fruit bearing, and it needs to be understood so it is not confused. The undisciplined vine, like the one I showed you yesterday, is still a vine in my vineyard. Similarly is the way a wayward or undisciplined son or daughter in God's family is still His child. The story of the Prodigal Son was Jesus' illustration of this point in His parable. A wild vine such as you saw in my vineyard is overgrown with old, non-productive branches that have turned to old wood, and can produce little meaningful fruit. Remember that old wood on a vine produces only leaves, but no grapes. There is so much entanglement of the old wood on the vine that disease comes into it, which further destroys any sparse fruit that might be produced later in the season. But it can be corrected."

Gabe paused as he took a breath and continued, "If I want to make the uncared-for vine productive,

I will have to do some major cutting and training to prepare it for pruning. Remember that I prune the branches on the trellis for the benefit of bearing more fruit. The ones I've trained have been formed through the years and have become consistently productive. Even so, I must continue to prune them each season for them to bear more fruit. But the uncared-for vine and its branches cannot be pruned like the others are, not at first. First, I have to cut and rip out a lot of bad growth from the vine. I have to cut most of the branches off the vine to even find the basic structure. After I am through, it looks almost as if I've killed it. In some cases, it might be killed by someone who doesn't know what he is doing. If a vine could experience pain, it would cry out and protest that I am ruthless. But I will never do more to it than it can handle, for I love it and have good plans for it. Still I must cut deeply so that the vine can be taken to the next steps to be nurtured, formed, and made into a productive vine."

Gabe had set it up and was now making the correlation: "Now consider this connection, for

there is a difference with the pruning of the Lord
and the discipline of the Lord, just like my work on
the undisciplined vine. Like my work on this wild
vine, God's discipline helps us by the necessary
removal of habitual sin and independence that
separates us. This pruning must be done before
we can begin our journey to close proximity with
Him and eventually become fruit producers."
Gabe went on by asking and answering his own
question, "Why is this? It is because God is holy,
and because we cannot bring our practice of sin
into a holy relationship and abide in Him.
Therefore, the purpose of the discipline of the Lord
is to help us identify and give up the sinful
conditions that keep us from coming closer to
Him. On the other hand, God's pruning is
because we are already close to Him. As Jesus
indicated, we are pruned because we are bearing
fruit so that we can bear even more fruit. God's
discipline helps us get into a right relationship with
Him, because some sort of practice of sin is
preventing it. At some point we as God's children
all have to be disciplined. It is the way our Father
gets us to understand that His holiness must be

respected, if we are to enjoy His holy presence in our life. Without God's discipline, we are just like that wild grape vine I showed you: independent, self-centered, and addicted to sin. Here's what scripture tells us." Gabe then opened his Bible to Hebrews 12: 3-11 and read,

Consider him who endured from sinners such hostility against himself, so that you may not grow weary or fainthearted. In your struggle against sin you have not yet resisted to the point of shedding your blood. And have you forgotten the exhortation that addresses you as sons?
My son, do not regard lightly the discipline of the Lord, nor be weary when reproved by him.
For the Lord disciplines the one he loves,
and chastises every son whom he receives.

It is for discipline that you have to endure. God is treating you as sons. For what son is there whom his father does not discipline? If you are left without discipline, in which all have participated, then you are illegitimate children and not sons. Besides this, we have had earthly fathers who disciplined us and we respected them. Shall we not much more be subject to the Father of spirits and live? For they disciplined us for a short time as it seemed best to them, but he disciplines us for our good, that we may share his holiness. For the moment all discipline seems painful rather than pleasant, but later it yields the peaceful fruit of righteousness to those who have been trained by it."

Gabe closed his Bible and looked over his reading glasses at me and asked, "Do you understand why I showed you the comparison?" He went on without my answer, "It is to teach you that sometimes you may be in a right place with the Lord but be made aware of an aspect of your life that hinders your fruit bearing. The Lord shows you this area and you must give it up, or it will limit your fruitfulness. This is the proper response to pruning. However, if you are holding onto a sinful practice, it is God's work to help you turn from that condition. That is His discipline. You must deal with that condition to go any further in your walk with Christ, for it will always hinder your intimacy with Him. Whether it is pruning or discipline the two are given to us by the Lord for different reasons, and yet sometimes they feel the same when we go through it."

"How will I know the difference?" I asked.

Gabe answered, "One of the great benefits of living in close proximity with Christ by abiding in Him is that we learn His voice. Rarely are we left in the dark about a hindrance to fruit bearing if our soul is healthy. Our problem is that we often do not want to readily give up something we value. The short answer is He will let you know what stands in the way, if you will diligently seek His answer to your question. Then it is simply a matter of obedience to give it over to Him."

When we live in an abiding relationship with the Lord we become more sensitive to sin and we tend to see discipline and pruning more clearly for what they are. Before we get there, however, we are often dull to a particular hinderance in our life. The discipline of the Lord encourages us to identify that sin and give it up. After some necessary, painful discipline, we become so challenged by the Lord's correction that we begin to see our sin and cry out for His forgiveness and restoration. Then the stranglehold of the enemy begins to lose its grip, as we release and repent of that which He reveals to us. It is also a necessary step toward an abiding relationship with Him."

Gabe continued, "If my nurtured vines could talk, they would say that they are familiar with their vinedresser's tender yet effective pruning. It takes time, but they become familiar with my touch and quickly adapt to what has been removed that will help them produce more fruit. On the other hand, the wild, undisciplined vine would cry out in pain, for a drastic change is initially very painful. However, the vinedresser has no less love or vision for his wild grapevine than his trained vine. It is the same with the Father and His children. There is no greater or less love from the Father when He disciplines or prunes us. It depends on what we need. Look at the story of the prodigal son and his father. The father never lost his love for his wayward son, and he welcomed him back with open arms. God will likewise never give up on His child. That is our Vinedresser."

Gabe's words of wisdom made it so clear to me the delicate yet thorough work of the Lord to help His man or woman come into an abiding relationship with Him. I felt I had a better foundation to ask some more questions, which I continued to do.

8 | Fruit *Described*

I now understood what healthy grapes look like on a vine and how they are produced. But it was still unclear to me what the fruit Jesus was speaking of looks like. So that was my next question to Gabe. He answered me by saying,

"How do I describe the fruit that comes from abiding in Christ? Well to begin with, it is more than we would expect or likely understand. The Lord keeps showing me more each day how His fruit grows and reproduces in the life of His disciple. For instance, years ago when I first read the passage about fruit in John 15, I thought

Jesus was referencing lives that would be turned toward Him through me. Therefore, I thought of it as a fruit of evangelism. Although it is true that our fruit in some way makes its way to the lost and dying world we live in, abiding in Christ is not simply to make us better evangelizers. There is more. Like the flower and fruit on a vine, the fruit of our intimate relationship with Jesus is a fragrance and a taste the Vine produces. There is a name for it. Do you know what it is?" Gabe asked. I shook my head. He responded, "It is called the 'fruit of the Spirit.'" We read about it together in Galatians 5:22,

But the fruit of the Spirit is love, joy,
peace, forbearance, kindness, goodness,
faithfulness, gentleness and self-control.

Gabe continued, "You need to understand what is being said here. The Apostle Paul is not telling us these are character qualities we can achieve through self-discipline. It is a common mistake for Christians to read this verse and think of it as a goal to achieve each of these characteristics, and they try to do it through self-help studies, or plan to mark these things off as accomplished. We cannot achieve these characteristics like that. In fact it is impossible, but at the same time possible."

I was confused, because I thought it was up to me to change myself to achieve these things. After all, most real change comes from discipline and perseverance, or so I thought.

Gabe could tell I was perplexed and said, "I didn't say it was impossible to have these characteristics. I said it is impossible if we feel that we as humans can achieve them. Here is the truth often overlooked. Look at the verse carefully and make a note about whose fruit is being mentioned."

I reread the verse and sure enough, the passage was clear. The characteristics mentioned are actually the characteristics of the Spirit. It is His fruit. Gabe then said, "This fruit is actually the personality and characteristics of the Holy Spirit, which is also true of Jesus and the Father. If we want to know what Jesus was like in person, these characteristics would describe Him."

"Well, Gabe," I asked, "If a human cannot achieve these characteristics, how is it possible for us to possess them, as you said?"

Gabe shot me a look that told me I'd asked the question he was hoping I would. Grinning he said, "Now you can understand the answer to your question about the fruit Jesus spoke of. Though the fruit will eventually lead to evangelism and discipleship and all manners of growth in the Body of Christ, the first fruit produced in a disciple of Christ is a transformed life. Though it is impossible for us to achieve the characteristics of Christ on our own, when we abide in Him the fruit of His Spirit begins to make His way to the surface of our life. and that is how this fruit is seen in our life. We receive these characteristics from Him. We don't attain or achieve them. We receive them. Ideally what is seen by our spouses, our friends and even

our enemies are those characteristics mentioned in Galatians 5:22."

Gabe went on, "Let's go back to the illustration of the vine and the fruit produced on it. The branch, which represents you and me, does the most important thing we can do. We stay connected to Jesus, the Vine. We remain connected with Him. We don't just visit Him. Just like the fruit produced on a vine is a natural process that the branch has nothing to do with, except to receive the flow of life from the vine, it is the same with a disciple who abides in Christ. With a grapevine the branch will eventually produce fruit from the flow that comes from the source. We know that fruit is a grape. It is not an apple or a pear or a watermelon but rather a grape, for the fruit is dictated by its source, which is a grapevine. It is the same with Jesus and His disciple."

After Gabe had laid his foundation he made his next point: "Doesn't it make sense that the fruit Jesus promised would look much like its Source? Doesn't it make sense that our life would begin to look more and more like Jesus, if we abide in Him and He is our Source? This is why I said it is possible that the fruit of the Spirit can also be evident in us. But it is completely dependent on Christ abiding in us and us in Him, and when this happens the Spirit works His way to the surface of our life and we display His characteristics. This fruit is evidence of an abiding relationship with Christ and it is in this relationship that the fruit Jesus mentioned begins by transforming us. However, it doesn't end there."

Gabe took a breath and a drink of coffee then said, "I said that the fruit Jesus mentioned is more than we would expect or likely understand. Let me give you some examples. I've seen corrupt lives turned to good. I've seen broken relationships mended. I've seen marriages saved. I've seen emotional wounds healed and forgiven. I've seen churches formed and reformed, and new ministries birthed. I've seen extreme generosity emerge from the changed lives of people who began to abide in Christ. I've seen communities changed. I've seen the greatest courage ever produced grow in a man, while at the same time the most tender and compassionate demeanor resided in the same guy. Talk about a contrast to the world's ways! I've seen religious status-quo be overridden by a movement of the Holy Spirit so strong that I thought I would lose my breath. I could go on and on about how broad and how extensively and how thoroughly a life is changed when a man or woman abides in Christ. To sum it up, when a life is so tremendously captivated by Jesus Christ that which is expressed from this person comes from a love relationship with Him that cannot remain silent. It must break out to the surface of our life. That is just a brief description of what the fruit looks like, but there is so much more."

I could tell that Gabe was speaking from his heart. This was not just religious chatter, for there was too much passion in the old man. I felt Gabe was leaving me the most important message that he could entrust to a person before he died. I think he had an idea that his time would be coming soon, and this was something that was important for him to help me see for myself. I say that it was important for him. But the truth is I can now see that Gabe entrusted to me the most valuable treasure I could have, and it has proven to be the most important thing I can pass along to generations who will follow me.

I've often asked myself what is the most valuable contribution I can make for my children, or grandchildren, or people that I might mentor. What can I do to prepare them for an uncertain future that may very well be full of great challenges, and likely challenges and trials unlike anything I've ever seen?   In every instance I have concluded that the best thing I can do is to help them understand and enter into an abiding relationship with Christ, for if they walk with Him they also have His constant companionship, input, and resources for anything that can come at them.

After my morning discussion with Gabe, we decided to take a break until after lunch. He took a little nap, for he was beginning to tire more easily each day. I went back to the stream for another round with the trout that were not very hungry the day before. The results were the same. They just would not bite what I was throwing at them. Before long I gave up and decided to reflect on what Gabe had shared with me on the porch that morning. So I returned to the base of the sycamore tree I had propped against the day before, opened my Bible and journal, and began to reflect on the wisdom that had just been downloaded to me. Here is what I recorded,

"Gabe has been very passionate about downloading the importance of abiding in Christ. I wonder if he thinks his time to transition to heaven is close, and it is an important last message to me? If this is true, then I better understand the context of why and how Jesus gave John 15 to the disciples. Jesus was emphatic, even repetitive with the word Abide / Remain. He said it numerous times. Why did He repeat himself? I think it was because He was only a few hours away from His crucifixion and death, and He must have wanted to pass along the most important last words He could give to His disciples. This alone makes me want to understand it better, for it was obviously important to Jesus and now Gabe. I've heard enough credible testimony from this man whom I trust to make me realize there is more than meets the eye on the concept of abiding in Christ. Later today I want to ask Gabe about some practical ways that I can learn to abide, and some things that might get in the way of it. All I know is that I'm highly motivated to seek Gabe's insight on this."

After I had written those words in my journal I asked God to open my eyes and heart to what He wanted to say to me through Gabe during the rest of my visit. I then closed my journal and walked back to Gabe's house.

9 | A Serious *Concern*

Neither Gabe nor I wanted lunch after the big
breakfast we had enjoyed that day. I wanted to
ask him about something I read in John 15:6 that
disturbed me. As soon as we took our seats on
the porch I asked, "Gabe, I've been tracking with
you and the concept of abiding in Christ. Jesus
said it is essential for bearing fruit, and when we
bear fruit we bring glory to the Father, and we
prove to be His disciples. This is clear to me. But
Jesus' exhortation takes a serious turn when He
says, "'If anyone does not abide in me he is
thrown away like a branch and withers; and the
branches are gathered, thrown into the fire, and

burned.'" This is frightening to me. Can you explain it? Is this person literally discarded? Gabe answered, "I don't know if I can. There are different opinions about this passage. However, everyone agrees, 'It is a serious concern.'"

Gabe went on. "I approach this verse by asking if abiding in Christ is optional or not? I suppose that is really the question, isn't it? Can a true believer or disciple of Christ be oblivious or dull to our need for Him to live within us when the Holy Spirit is at work to lead us to Him? I think not. I think it is the work of the Holy Spirit to convict us of our sins and to seek a relationship with Jesus Christ at the start of it all. But I also think it is the work of the Vinedresser to create in us a desire to abide in Him as well, for fruit bearing requires both. Regardless of our age or time of life, He works in us in such a way to create in us a desire to ultimately have an intimate, abiding relationship with Him. I believe this is a pattern. Unfortunately, many do not yield to this invitation or deep desire within their heart."

Gabe paused and thought before he spoke again.
"I think it is part of our original created nature to
desire this intimate connection with our Creator. It
was created in us. I believe I can look at everyone
I see and know that deep down he or she wants
to have this kind of intimate connection with their
Creator, even though they may not realize it. Like
the third seed in Jesus' parable of the four seeds,
their lives are so busy and hectic and conflicted
that they don't even realize their need, much less
that there could be something better for them.
Some people flat out reject Christ and in doing so
there is no hope for them. Some do not know the
way to Him. Others are satisfied with a status-quo
existence. There are many followers of Christ who
think of Christianity simply as rules, regulations
and a religious experience, and they reject Him
because of this. They do not understand that
true Christianity is not a religion but rather a
restored relationship, because Jesus has bridged
the great chasm between mankind and Holy God
and has given us the ability to be restored to our
lost intimacy with Him. For those who reject Christ
and refuse to allow Him to abide in them, their fate

has already been sealed. They are lost and will never escape the judgement that comes. It is similar to a branch on one of my vines that is sterile. I will cut it off and burn it up, for it will never bear fruit. It is not because it doesn't bear fruit that I destroy it. It is because it is lifeless and sterile and as a result can bear no fruit. Therefore, it can play no part in my vineyard. When we reject Jesus as our Lord and Savior, we reject Him abiding in us and there is a serious consequence. This verse can also be applied to people who claim to be Christians because of church affiliation, or good works, but Christ does not truly abide in them. In fact, Jesus Himself said,

"'Not everyone who says to me, "'Lord, Lord,'" will enter the kingdom of heaven, but the one who does the will of my Father who is in heaven. On that day many will say to me, "'Lord, Lord, did we not prophesy in your name, and cast out demons in your name, and do many mighty works in your name?'" And then will I declare to them, "'I never knew you; depart from me, you workers of lawlessness.'" Matthew 7:21-23 ESV

"This is why many scholars view your question about John 15:6 with a serious concern, for not only are those who outright refuse Him destined to perish, but also many people who might be religious, good, church going people will not enter the kingdom of heaven, because Christ does not abide in them. Their futures are mighty sorrowful. Although it seems like the Vine is rejecting them, the fact is they have rejected Him, and so they perish. This is what is being said in John 15:6."

I was feeling a little fear creeping into me, so I asked, "Gabe, how can we be sure? How can we know if Christ truly abides in us?"

Gabe answered, "Jesus said that when we bear much fruit we prove to be His disciples. But don't just look at the fruit itself as evidence, for just as there is a process for fruit to develop on the vine, it is the same with a follower of Christ. It might take more or less time than we expect, for after all the Vinedresser is in charge of the process, right?

Gabe continued, "Since Jesus used the grapevine to describe our abiding and fruit bearing relationship with Him, we might want to reconsider something I taught you about the process of becoming a fruit bearer. Remember this: Discipline comes before abiding, abiding comes before pruning, pruning comes before fruit, and fruit is the result of abiding. We are able to see our spiritual life through this process. If our relationship is real, then we will see these things occurring and it will tell us where we are in God's process of developing us."

"Concerning God's discipline, even though we are not bearing fruit at the time, His loving discipline proves that we are His children. His discipline is not to punish us, but rather to help us escape a sinful condition that we hold onto. Fruit is clearly the eventual result of abiding in Christ and Him in us. Therefore, abiding in Him is the only concern we have. Or if He is disciplining us, then that is our immediate concern. If we are being disciplined, then it becomes less about fruit in our life and more about being right with Him. The eventual fruit born in our life comes from His developing work in our life. The Spirit will be at work in you to help you with this. His wounds, snips, and cuts sometimes hurt. But they are always for our own good. You should remember this when it is happening. If you are troubled and concerned about where you are in all this, let your concern drive you to remove anything that hinders your walk with Christ. If it is sin, then that must be dealt with through sincere repentance and receiving His forgiveness. If you are blind to what it may be, ask God to show you. He will. Then you do your business with Him. Through all of these processes, whether it be pruning or discipline, the Holy Spirit invites us to draw closer to Him. This is how we move into close proximity with Him.

There is another thing I have observed. If a believer is living in sin, the Holy Spirit will make his or her life miserable until it is given up, for He cannot abide with sin. If there is no remorse, or no discipline being given to this person who professes to be a believer, I seriously doubt the Spirit is there. The Apostle John said it like this,

'No one born of God makes a practice of sinning, for God's seed abides in him; and he cannot keep on sinning, because he has been born of God. By this it is evident who are the children of God, and who are the children of the devil: whoever does not practice righteousness is not of God, nor is the one who does not love his brother.' 1 John 3:9-10

Keep in mind that John mentions the 'practice of sin.' He did not say being sin-free. We will stumble in sin, and God has a provision for that. But the 'practice of sin' is a habitual, repetitive sin without the holy remorse I speak of, and it is evidence that Christ does not abide in that person."

With this last statement Gabe had opened the door to my final question for the day. Now that I understood more about the fruit and the process of abiding, I wanted to know some obvious and not so obvious hindrances that get in the way of it.

10 | The *Invitation*

"Gabe, what are some hindrances that get in the way of my abiding in Christ?" I asked.

Gabe answered me: "The first thing you need to establish in your mind is that you are responding to the invitation Christ has offered you to come closer to Him, and the two of you abide together. It is not your original idea to pilgrimage to Him. It began with His pilgrimage to you. He initiated that journey to you at the cross and by His resurrection. He began to dwell in you at the time of your salvation. Therefore, from that time His Spirit has lived within you. He abides in you. He did His part. But His invitation to you now, as it was with His disciples in John 15, is to journey beyond your initial relationship with Him and to abide with Him in a deeper way. Many believers mistakenly think their spiritual lives are complete when they receive salvation, and they simply wait for heaven while doing their best to manage their sins. But it is much more. We have been given an opportunity to represent Christ to our world while becoming more Christ-like in the process. We have been given the opportunity to play a noble part in our King's outreach to a lost world. Now, let me address your question about hindrances in your journey to this deeper intimacy with God."

"An obvious hindrance is unrepentance and unforgiven sin. Remember, God is holy and sin is offensive to Him. We cannot abide in His presence if we do not respect this fact."

I had to interrupt Gabe. "Does that mean as long as I sin I cannot come closer to Him? How impossible would that be? As hard as I try not to, I still sin. Who in this world can completely cease

from sinning? Jesus could, but, how can I?" I
asked with surprising boldness. My confusion
gave Gabe a way to unpack his thoughts on God's
holiness, for I had some misunderstanding of it.
He led me to 1 Peter 1:13-15 and read,

Therefore, preparing your minds for action,
and being sober-minded, set your hope fully on
the grace that will be brought to you at the
revelation of Jesus Christ. As obedient
children, do not be conformed to the passions of
your former ignorance, but as he who called you is
holy, you also be holy in all your conduct, since it
is written, "You shall be holy, for I am holy.

Gabe followed these verses with, "The holiness of
God cannot be attained by mankind. God must
give us His holiness. This is why Jesus came and
died for us. He became the substitute holiness we
need by exchanging our sinful nature with His
holiness. He did so while we were still sinners, not
because we deserved it or earned it, but because
of His grace which is an unconditional gift. His
forgiveness and holiness are gracious gifts. Now

if this salvation comes to us as an unconditional gift while we were yet sinners, do we have to now earn it to keep it? If so, it would not be grace. It would be a conditional pardon. So, when Peter encourages God's family to be holy because God is holy, he also clearly points out that our hope rests entirely on God's grace. Another way of saying it is that our salvation comes by God's grace and it stays with us by God's grace. That is why Peter said for us to "set your hope fully on the grace that will be brought to you at the revelation of Jesus Christ." Our hope is in His grace alone when we face Him at our resurrection. That is how we are made holy and have the beginnings of a relationship with Him. Now let's talk about abiding with Holy God."

"We cannot enjoy a deeper intimate fellowship with God if unforgiven sin abides in us, for He is still holy. Talk about a hindrance? We cannot be casual or nonchalant about our sin and come to the place of abiding in Christ. This is why He disciplines His children, so that we will come to see our sin, turn from it, and then move closer to Him."

"What if I stumble in sin?" I asked. "Sometimes I have sinful thoughts I embrace before I even realize it. Sometimes I am weaker than normal or simply have a bad day and slip into sin. What about these situations?"

Gabe answered, "There is a difference in slipping up compared to the ongoing practice of habitual sin. The practice of habitual sin is a consistent choice that we must make. It is not a slip up. It is planned action on our part rather than hasty reaction. We will all stumble, for that is the simple reality of our nature and the world we live in. When we do stumble we can repent of it, seek God's forgiveness, receive His forgiveness as promised, and then press on as a clean and forgiven child of God. Forgiveness is God's provision to keep us connected to the Vine even though we have sinned. But the practice of sin is much more of a problem for us." Gabe let his words linger until I probed,

"How is it a greater problem?"

He answered, "The practice of sin tells us that we have not yet come to grips with our hypocrisy. We think we can fool other people and hide the rotting condition of our souls, but God knows it. If our souls are not crying out within us and we feel no guilt or disturbance over our habitual sin, then there is a serious doubt as to whether we have ever truly known Jesus Christ. That is the greater problem. You see, as I said before, the Spirit of God lives within a true follower of Christ, no matter what his or her condition is with sin. He does not leave us even though we may stray from Him. He is faithful even though we may temporarily betray our relationship with Him, for our relationship has been established on His grace and not our being sin-free. I repeat, you may be sure the Spirit will make life miserable for one of His children who practices a sinful condition habitually. The absence of that misery is a good indication of what is missing, which is a genuine relationship with the Holy Spirit who lives within a true follower of Jesus Christ."

Gabe paused as if to change the subject.
However, it was as if he thought of something
more I needed to understand before moving on.

"Do not confuse your concept of personal holiness
with the only way of being made right with God. If
you do, you may fall into legalism and a critical
spirit toward others who do not meet your criteria
for holiness. True holiness is not our being sin-free
but rather that we sin less. It is the holiness of
Jesus alone that makes us holy with God. If we
go down a path that measures ourselves and
others based on a perceived requirement of being
sin-free, then we will embrace a spirit of
Pharisaism. Then, like them, we will think we can
perfect ourselves to heaven and that we are free
to criticize those who are failing. What pride this
spirit shows! And yet such a person rarely sees
his own pride as sin. The holiness Peter speaks of
in this verse is the sincere dedication to live a life
that honors God. It is a dedicated, consecrated
life, but not a perfect one. We give Him who we
were, what we are, and what we will be, which
includes our imperfections, our failures, our sins,

and our desire to be more like Him. Holiness for you and me means we submit to God's leadership and allow Him to nurture us into Christlikeness. In the process we will gain ground against sin. But we will also lose a little ground along the way. During this process sin will lose its appeal, for Jesus is growing more significant in us each day. Eventually we sin less. But we will never be sin-free."

Gabe's tone became even more serious. "Listen to me. We are no more or less holy when we begin our relationship with Jesus Christ, or when we mature in our walk with Him. He has already made us holy by His gracious atonement for our sins in the past, in the present, and in the future. It was not by good works or high moral character that we received this relationship with Him. We are justified by His grace, sanctified by it, and will one day be glorified by it. That is the completeness of God's grace and what it means for us. Never embrace a false view of sin-free holiness, for we can never be good enough to be justified before Holy God. But we can grow into sinning less and that is the path you must seek. God will never demand your perfection. But He does require the consecration of your life. When you make that commitment, then He can nurture you into Christ-likeness."

"Gabe," I asked, "Are there things that are not sinful or willfully disobedient acts, but that could be a hindrance to a deeper, abiding relationship with Christ?"

Gabe answered. "Yes. Consider that even the vines I prune each year would return to their wild growth if I did not prune them. Even a Christian who is doing well with his life could allow wrong things to come into his life and not know it, for it is our nature to adapt to our world and it is always invading our walk with Christ. Even if we are not holding onto a sinful condition in our lives, we can still have hindrances that block our way to a closer walk with Christ. This is why the Spirt prunes us, so that we can see those hindrances and willingly give them over to Christ."

"What are some examples of hindrances?" I asked.

Gabe answered, "One hindrance might be something like a conflict in a relationship or an activity that we can see no harm in that we must give up. God sees His future plans for us and it may require an adjustment. It may be an old wound from the past or an unresolved thought about someone who hurt us that is moving toward bitterness. Although it might not yet be sin, it could move us into sin. Can you see how God's pruning is used to prevent this? It is much like my work in pruning to prevent disease in my vines."

Gabe continued, "It may be a lack of verbal self-restraint that takes us into gossip or slander. We don't see a problem. But that is because we do not see it through God's eyes. By pruning us God gives us His perspective, and His perspective helps us bear greater fruit with people who may be offended by our loose tongues. There are numerous other things that might not be seen as sin, but that could lead to sin. It could be something about trust we need to learn, and the Lord allows a condition that requires us to trust Him more. This pruning draws us closer to Him as we begin to trust Him more. There's a whole lot of good that comes from a deeper trust, and it is the work of God to help us experience them. That is His agenda. He wants to bless us more greatly than we can imagine. But it requires our trust. Those are just a few examples of hindrances to our abiding with Christ, which will also hinder our fruit as well."

Gabe had done a marvelous job of opening my eyes to the love God gives with His pruning and disciplining of His children. I felt much more comfortable, for I could see that either would always lead to His blessings. After our discussion I told Gabe I wanted to give the river one more chance to provide us fish for dinner. I would be leaving the next morning to return home. To my surprise Gabe said he wanted to join me. So, we headed to the river.

11 | Becoming A *Laborer*

I gathered my fly fishing equipment and walked down the path to the river that ran through the back of Gabe's property. I noticed he took his old cane fishing pole from the place where it hung on the back porch. He also took an old coffee can for worms. Gabe told me that fly fishing is mighty pretty, but it was not his thing.

We stopped at a compost pile that had been rotting for years. He made one swipe of the rake that he kept there and uncovered a half-dozen nice-sized worms. He put the worms in his coffee can and said, "Let's go get supper."

When we got to the river's edge, Gabe sat on a fallen log while he caught his breath. I could tell that the things he could do so easily before were now clearly tiring him. He told me to go ahead and start my fishing.

Even though I was a grown man with my own children, I still wanted my old mentor to see me cast my flies and to approve. I stood a short way in the water out in front of him, looked behind, and saw that a tree would tangle my fly if I used a standard cast. So, I laid out a perfect roll cast while imagining a round of applause for doing a great job. The problem is it didn't catch a fish. In fact, I would continue to throw those beautiful casts for about an hour, and no matter where I placed the fly there were no bites. I then heard Gabe stand up and groan a little when he did so. I looked back and could see him unwinding the monofilament line from around his bamboo pole. As he walked toward me I got out of the way, for I knew we had both had enough of my fishing attempts for the day.

Gabe got to the water's edge, baited his

hook with a worm, and then looked at me with a wink and said, "About four nice fish should do us, right?" He then threw his bait to the same rock I had been working and immediately caught a beautiful rainbow trout. With three more worms and three more placements of the bait, Gabe had caught our supper. He handed the worms to me and said, "Take these worms and put them back in the compost pile so you can use them when you come back. By the way, you clean the fish and I'll fry them up tonight." I couldn't argue with Gabe's offer.

Gabe looked at my fly rod and then at me while saying, "You look mighty pretty throwing that thing. But if you want to catch fish you might need to do what works instead of what looks good."

I looked at my fly rod outfit that had cost me hundreds of dollars and then at Gabe's bamboo cane pole he had cut from the river bank. I shook my head and asked, "Where can I get one of those things? Can I have yours?" We both had a deep laugh while we walked back up the trail leading to Gabe's house. He had done it to me again.

I cleaned the fish while Gabe heated the

cooking oil in the cast iron fry skillet. He began his preparation by making his hush puppies, wonderful, savory, deep-fried balls that go hand in hand with fried fish. He made a cornmeal batter using his own recipe of buttermilk, corn meal, and flour, along with a chopped sweet onion, salt, pepper and his secret seasoning. Gabe introduced it to me, and I can no longer have fried fish without it now. After he dropped the balls of cornmeal into the skillet of hot oil, he coated the fish with similar ingredients. He added a small amount of grits to the coating to make the fish extra crispy, which we both preferred. When the hush puppies were finished cooking, he dropped the fish in. His objective was to time everything so that all would be hot and crispy when he served it. As was the case with all the other meals he cooked for me, they finished perfectly. He also cooked some vegetables to go with the fish, and lastly placed a jar of his pickled green tomatoes on the table to join the other dishes. The relish added a sweet finish to every bite of fish and hush puppy. When we prayed and began eating, I was reminded of so many fine meals with the old man.

The fish fry was as good as ever. But my time with Gabe would be one of my favorite memories with him, for it would be our last meal together.

When we finished our dinner and I had cleaned the dishes and the kitchen, we went back to our rocking chairs on the front porch. The sun had set below the horizon and the night sounds of the country were waking up. Like the night before, a whippoorwill began its call. We both listened silently for a while until Gabe spoke up.

"When my children and I sat on this very porch listening to the night sounds, I told them the whippoorwill had a language, and if they listened closely they could make out what he was saying. I would tell them the bird was saying, 'Chip-fell-out-of-the-white-oak.' They would ask me why the whippoorwill said that, and I would tell them it was up to them to figure it out. That's when their imaginations took off. You should have heard some of their conversations! Katherine and I would be out of sight listening to all their theories and explanations. We laughed, we cried, but we knew we were raising them right."

"How often do you see them?" I asked.

"Several times a year. But they all live a long way away and have their families and careers to consider. So it's hard for them to come as often as they would like. I'm not neglected by them at all. They didn't like farming and I sure didn't want for them the same hard life we had. That is why we led them toward education and careers. We had them in our home for a time and, as God's steward of those children, we got them started in life and in their walks with Him. We all love each other. We are close. We all live in a good place both relationally and physically. I am happy for them and they are for me. But the most important thing is they all know Jesus, and that means we have the promise of a relationship with each other that will never end. For that reason we can be at peace with our lives."

Gabe paused and said, "Let's recapture what you've learned before I share one more thing with you. I want you to condense what you've learned into an explanation of Christ's teaching on abiding in Him and tell me what it means to you." Gabe waited for my answer. I thought for a few minutes and ventured,

"I see that Jesus is telling me He has a plan for my life. This plan begins by joining with Him so that He can abide in me. This is what it means to receive Jesus into my heart. At that point I am saved, and He begins to abide in me. He does His part in the abiding relationship. At that point I am made holy and secured for salvation. But there is more beyond that point, and this is what I didn't understand. He wants to make me into a man after His own heart. He wants me to become more like Him, and it is His work for the rest of my life to reform me after His own character and values. His characteristics, called the 'fruit of the Spirit,' slowly become mine when I abide in Him. His Spirit takes over and it becomes more of Him and less of me. It is a surrender of my old life to be made into a new man."

I continued, "I see the illustration Jesus gave in

John 15 to be both His plan and the process for making me into this man. There is necessary discipline for correction to get me started, and then pruning which is an act of surrender of something getting in the way of His plan. The fruit produced from our relationship is a confirmation of the Holy Spirit's work to help me abide more deeply in Christ. I see this clearly. It now makes sense to me."

I went on, "The fruit is extensive and varies. But it all tracks back to one thing. It is Jesus who is producing this fruit through me. It is not from myself or my abilities. It is His work through me. For that reason, I need to remain in Him and I need to remove any hindrance that gets in the way of it. The hindrances are primarily my responsibility to remove so that I can move closer to Christ. He will reveal them to me if I seek Him, and as I surrender them and move closer to Him the fruit is better and more abundant. The fruit is always best when we are closest to Him. That is something that is illustrated with the vine, the branch, and the fruit."

I then asked Gabe, "Tell me how you abide in Christ?"

He pondered, then replied: "It is simple now. It took some time before I surrendered all my junk and wounds and self. But eventually it became a daily walk with Him. I wake every day and pray, 'Lord here I am. Take what you want of me and use it. I just ask You to let me walk with You every minute today.' I listen. I respond to His leading. I trust that He will use me for His purposes. That is abiding for me, for He is faithful to do just what I asked of Him. Initially I had to begin a reorientation by studying scripture. But I could not camp out on just having Bible knowledge. I needed to apply His word to my life and allow His words to lead me. His word went through my mind and into my heart. If it didn't go there I would not understand what it means to abide in Him, and I would think it is only about knowledge. I still go to His word, for there is much more to learn. I know I was invited to a relationship with our Living God, and I go there to Him through His word. But His word is only a map and not a destination. For that reason, we must understand that there is more to be learned on the relational level with Him. This is when we move toward the second part of abiding. He is already abiding in me. But I must now journey forward to do my part and abide in Him. Jesus said, 'Abide in me, and I in you.' There are two critical components in our abiding relationship with Him. He does His part, but we must surrender ourselves to Him to do our part. I want to remain in this intimacy with Him. That is my daily walk and that is what abiding means to me."

He continued, "Do you understand why Jesus is growing us up by drawing us to closer to Him? Jesus asked for us to pray for laborers, for the harvest is great and the laborers are few. Jesus told us we need laborers. Would you like to know what a laborer looks like?" I nodded that I did.

"Jesus referenced a harvest, which would be understood by a culture that depended on crops to live. They would understand the preparation of the soil, the sowing of the seed, the nurturing of the plants, and the eventual harvest and storing of the crops. All the people involved with the harvest from start to finish were considered laborers. Each had his or her own specialty concerning the production of a crop. But all their work, no matter how individualized it would be, was focused on the harvest. Jesus said to pray for laborers, for the preparatory work had been done by Him and the prophets before Him, and the harvest was ready. So, what is a laborer today?"

Gabe answered his own question: "Here's what I think. I believe the laborer today is the Body of Christ and each member of the Body of Christ has a special role to play. Each of us has our own spiritual gifts, talents, unique experiences with Christ, and tremendous abilities that can serve our King. A laborer is able to reproduce after himself and extend the harvest to greater fields. But to use all of those abilities to serve our King in His harvest, the unique abilities within us must be enabled. This empowerment only happens when we abide in Jesus Christ. Remember what He said? 'As the branch cannot bear fruit by itself, unless it abides in the vine, neither can you, unless you abide in me.'

I am concerned that the Church does not understand these principles. As a result, most of our good efforts are frustrated by our human limitations rather than enabled by the power that should flow from abiding in Jesus. We have to help other believers understand how important this promise is and how it helps us carry out His mission. We are enabled to be laborers by our intimate walk with Him. Jesus was adamant with His disciples that they must abide in Him to do the great work in the great harvest that would follow. It is the same with you and me and all Christians today. We must abide in Him. We must remain in Him. You must abide in Him." As he said those last words, He looked at me more intently as if to make an important point. Gabe directed me to 1 Corinthians 13:1-8 and I followed along. He pointed out, "The Apostle Paul wrote to the Church in Corinth that even though they had a bunch of spiritual gifts and abilities, those gifts would accomplish nothing without love. The kind of love Paul was referencing is seen only in the fruit of the Spirit. This love comes only from God. It changes people and enables us to engage our unique ministry gifts. It is one of the promised benefits of abiding in Christ. It is how a laborer is formed, and man, we need them more than ever before. God's love is unleashed through us and it affects people in a big way."

After Gabe and I chatted for about an hour more, I could tell he was worn out from the day's activities. He needed some sleep, so I encouraged him to go to bed which he gladly did. It was still early in the evening, so I decided to take a walk up the road a short piece, enjoy the nighttime sky, and reflect on the day. My head was spinning with new information that I needed to process. But there were things that were also lining up and beginning to make sense to me, at least from a spiritual perspective. It occurred to me that the path Christ invites us to follow rarely makes sense to a fallen world or people who do not know Him. Scripture says those without the Spirit do not accept the things that come from Him. They even think it is foolishness. My eyes were now being opened to truths that were hidden before, and I was growing in excitement about my future in Christ as never before. I was now beginning to see more clearly what I had been given in Jesus Christ and also what was missing in me. I now wanted to abide deeply in Christ to find it. I lifted my hands heavenward and cried out, "Lord, here I am. Take what You want of me and use it. I just ask You to let me walk with You every minute tonight and for the rest of my life."

After this prayer, I realized I had prayed the same prayer Gabe had. It might have been the impression he made on me without my realizing it. But more so, I think it was a simple heart's cry of a son spoken to his Father in Heaven. Nothing fancy or wordy. Just simple, to the point, and heartfelt. Gabe and I were on the same track.

After my prayer I walked back to the house and went to bed. In a few moments I was asleep.

12 | Sifting

The next morning after breakfast, Gabe and I gathered on the porch to finish up a final point he wanted to make before I returned home. We took our coffee to our chairs. As he sipped from his cup he paused and asked, "If you sum up all you've learned about the discipline of the Lord and the necessity to abide in Him, can you give me three words that describe what He is doing in His child's life with those two processes?"

I thought for a moment and said, "He's transforming us."

"I see it that way as well," Gabe responded. "Our Vinedresser, the Lord, is at work transforming us from the fatherless orphans we once were into a royal priesthood that carries his name and serves His purposes. Each one of us is under His delicate scrutiny and carefully laid out plan of development.   All His work in our lives is moving us toward a point where we can make the best and most important contribution of our lives for His purposes."

We can stand in the way of His work if we do not submit to Him, and many do not submit, and for that reason those who resist His development process will never reach the potential they could have. They can still have their adoption by Him, by His grace. But they still think of themselves as orphans. They fail to mature and be transformed into a new identity He wants to give them. They fail to bear the great fruit their lives could potentially produce. There is one more point I want to make concerning God's development process for some people. It does not come from John 15, but it is related to a special preparation for some of God's children, especially those who will be carrying a larger ministry burden." Gabe had my attention.

"Not all people will be taken to the length of development this special attention provides. What I'm speaking of is the most difficult form of development and preparation that some of us can face. It might even be considered a combination of discipline and pruning and an evil abuse by a strange opposition toward our lives. It is a work of Satan that God permits to come to certain members in His family, to challenge a man or woman's faith so thoroughly that it has the potential to even destroy his or her faith. It is painful. But whatever illusion or weakness of faith we once had is replaced by a faith so completely pure that it takes this person to a special place of service for God. The illusions of grandeur are filtered out of our lives if we stand the test, and God will replace them with a great work only He can build. It is called sifting.

If you will read in the Bible where the word sifting is used, you will see that it has to do with testing that ultimately prepares a person for something God has planned. You will also see that the sifting of a person is done by Satan and is allowed by God. Satan must request permission or otherwise he cannot bring this sifting to us. Let me read you these verses about it. Gabe turned to Luke 22:31-32 and read,

Simon, Simon, Satan has asked to sift all of you as wheat. But I have prayed for you, Simon, that your faith may not fail. And when you have turned back, strengthen your brothers.

Gabe continued, "Notice that permission must be granted by God to sift a member of His family. If we stand the test, the result will produce something of great value to our lives and our work for God. In the case of Peter and the other disciples, it was to prepare them for the great ministry of building the Church that would shortly follow their sifting. They had to be prepared, and this sifting was the final phase in their preparation. It may happen to you and I want you to be prepared if it comes."

This last statement sent a chill up my spine even though it was a warm morning. I wasn't ready for Gabe's last words following a great weekend. I didn't want it to end with such a sobering warning. Yet he went on,

"This doesn't mean God doesn't love you. The fact is He is entrusting your faith to a greater test to make it deeper and stronger because He does love you and wants to use you for something special. To do this He must get you out of the way, and sifting is simply a process to accomplish His purpose. He is clear that no trial or temptation will overcome you, for He will be at your side. Always remember this when you are in such a trial. The sifting will force you closer to Him and this is where the greatest fruit is formed in your life. Right next to Him. The process of sifting takes you there and it is there that a great work can be done through your life. If you are chosen for a greater ministry work such as I speak of, it will likely be preceded by sifting. Do not be afraid of it, for God has the ultimate say. He is sovereign.

Jesus told Peter to strengthen his brothers

after his own sifting. You can readily see the purpose and the credibility Jesus knew would come to Peter when he passed through his test. That will be your mission as well, should you be sifted. This is where your spiritual gifts and experiences with God become empowered as never before to do an even greater work in making disciples. I'm not saying you will be sifted. I'm only saying that if you are, it is for a greater work God is inviting you to and as with all the other processes of development He uses in our lives, this is just one of them, for certain people."

I asked, "Gabe, do I need to ask God to sift me?"

Gabe answered, "I don't think we need to ask the Lord to prepare us or use us in a certain way if we are committed to whatever He asks of us. I think He wants us to simply trust Him and whatever process He uses to prepare us. I do think we should ask to be used by Him all of our days to bring Him glory. This is the heart of a consecrated life. Let Him determine what that looks like and how to get you there. Your only concern is to abide in Him and let Him do the rest. Your daily walk with Him will take you where He wants you, and your abiding in Him will prepare you for what you face. By walking and abiding, your life will turn out better than you could ever design for yourself."

Gabe and I remained silent for a while, until I rose from the chair and told him it was time for me to return home. With that, we both walked to my truck and started the customary "so longs" we always said. But today was different.

13 | My Last *So Long*

I noticed a somber look in Gabe's eyes. I felt a sense of remorse but did not know why. So, I asked him,

"Gabe, tell me what's going on with you   I feel there is something you are not telling me. I've noticed you were not your normal, spunky self and there seemed to be a sense of urgency to share your message this weekend. Are you okay?"

Gabe looked at me with the eyes of a spiritual father. He looked beyond my questions and into the heart of my concern, and answered:

"I have a sense of great joy and anticipation, but also concern for some of my loved ones and friends. I feel the Lord has prepared me that any day now He may take me home. I am ready for that. More than ready. But there is a lingering thought that some are not ready for what they will face in life and are not prepared for the challenges. They do not understand the things I have shared with you, and they have little interest in pursuing a closer walk with Christ. I feel they are in danger. I fear many homes and families will be broken apart, lives will be ruined by idols and addictions, and a cultural Christianity will develop in this country that waters down God's guidance so much that it will no longer have much impact. All of this is done so as not to offend other religions or non-believers or atheists or those with political agendas. But they walk away from the truth. They walk away from Jesus. And what hope will they have if they do? Perhaps this is what you are picking up on? Yes, I have a sense of urgency especially with someone like you, whom I love like a son. That is why I wanted to give you the most important message I can give you at this time of my life, and in this stage of yours."

"Well, father Gabe," I answered with affection and with a smile, "I think your concern now needs to be mine and every other disciple of Christ's. It's not your concern alone to carry. I pledge to you that I will carry forward the message about abiding immediately, and I will make it my intention to go there myself. I promise this to you."

Changing the subject, I said, "By the way, we didn't plant your garden as I had planned. But you did clearly deliver the message you wanted, and I receive it gladly. I'll have to get on that garden when I return."

When I got in the truck and closed the door, Gabe was standing right next to it, looking at me through the window. I looked at him one last time and

said, "Any last words for me, my dear friend, before I go?"

Gabe reached through the window with both hands and put a hand on each side of my face. He focused his eyes into mine and smiled a smile that only he could give. He then said:

"Abide my son, abide. That is the most important message I can give to you."

With those last words I drove down his gravel drive, turned on the paved road, and headed home. As I drove home I had a melancholic feeling that this would be the last time I would see Gabe. Sure enough, three days later he died. His body was discovered by the neighbor who checked on him every day. He had died peacefully in his sleep. We would hold his funeral a few days later in the nearby town, in the burned-down church he had helped restore.

        The last weekend I had with Gabe marked the beginning of a new direction for me. This new direction was built on my continued self-feeding in God's word and the biblical foundation it gave me. Beyond that foundation, I would take more deliberate steps in my personal abandonment and absolute trust in the Lord. I would let go of illusions that I could somehow control the outcome of mine or my family's life, and I would give more deliberate attention to trusting the Lord more deeply. This would help me begin a true walk with Jesus, as Gabe had suggested, and it would take me on a life adventure with Jesus that has been better than I could ever describe. I can only say that it has led me to the desires of my heart, for this is what abiding in Christ does.

One of those desires became reality several months after Gabe's death. His children allowed my wife and me to purchase Gabe's farm just as he had left it. It became a frequent weekend home for my family, and we used it for the discipleship ministry that developed around our walks with Christ. When I retired we moved there permanently. After moving there I would discover there was even more to Gabe and his influence than I knew. When I got to know the people of the valley, I heard their stories. They had all said Gabe was a real hero to them and for some very good reasons. I learned their stories and saw how his life blended into theirs and why he meant so much to them. I look forward to telling you those stories. But if there is one thing that Gabe and I want you to remember from this story, it is this: ABIDE, ABIDE, ABIDE!

Want to read more about Gabe and his influence? Find it in the next adventure about Gabe's valley in Compelled by Grace. This book can be purchased from the Influencers bookstore, or digitally through Kindle Books.